Lewis and Clark

Captains Lewis and Clark visit with a group
of Indians.

JUNIOR ■ WORLD ■ BIOGRAPHIES

Lewis and Clark

REBECCA STEFOFF

CHELSEA JUNIORS

a division of CHELSEA HOUSE PUBLISHERS

Chelsea House Publishers
EDITOR-IN-CHIEF: Remmel Nunn
MANAGING EDITOR: Karyn Gullen Browne
COPY CHIEF: Mark Rifkin
PICTURE EDITOR: Adrian G. Allen
ART DIRECTOR: Maria Epes
ASSISTANT ART DIRECTOR: Noreen Romano
MANUFACTURING MANAGER: Gerald Levine
SYSTEMS MANAGER: Lindsey Ottman
PRODUCTION MANAGER: Joseph Romano
PRODUCTION COORDINATOR: Marie Claire Cebrián

JUNIOR WORLD BIOGRAPHIES

SENIOR EDITOR: Kathy Kuhtz

Staff for LEWIS AND CLARK
SENIOR COPY EDITOR: Laurie Kahn
PICTURE RESEARCHER: Joan Beard
SENIOR DESIGNER: Marjorie Zaum
COVER ILLUSTRATION: Bill Donahey

First Printing

1 3 5 7 9 8 6 4 2

Library of Congress Cataloging-in-Publication Data
Stefoff, Rebecca
   Lewis and Clark/Rebecca Stefoff.
     p. cm.—(Junior world biographies)
   Summary: A biography of the two men who led the two-and-one-half year
expedition that explored the Louisiana Purchase territory and the Pacific
Northwest from St. Louis to the mouth of the Columbia River.
ISBN 0-7910-1750-8
   1. Lewis, Meriwether, 1774–1809—Juvenile literature. 2. Clark, William,
1770–1838—Juvenile literature. 3. Explorers—West (U.S.)—Biography—
Juvenile literature. 4. Lewis and Clark Expedition (1804–6)—Juvenile
literature. [1. Lewis, Meriwether, 1774–1809. 2. Clark, William.
1770–1838. 3. Explorers. 4. Lewis and Clark Expedition (1804–6)
5. West (U.S.)—Discovery and exploration.] I. Title. II. Series.
F592.7.S69 1992
978′02′0922—dc20
[B]   91-12561
AC   CIP

Contents

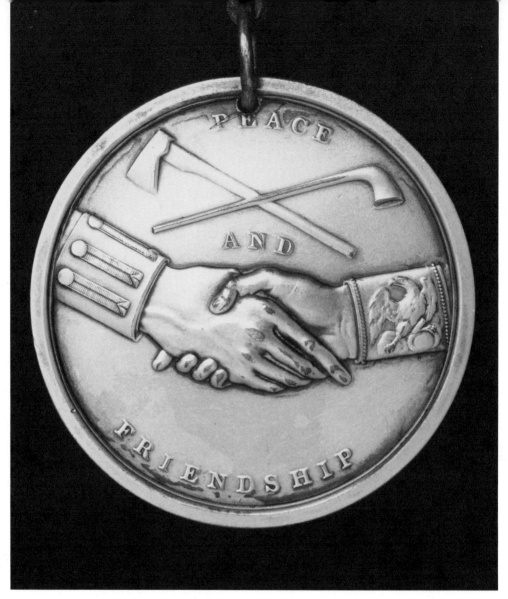

A copy of one of the peace medals President Jefferson asked Lewis and Clark to give to the Indians they met on their trip west.

1

Captains of
the Wilderness

A few years before the American colonies went to war with Britain to win their freedom, two boys were born in the colony of Virginia. Their names were Meriwether Lewis and William Clark. They grew up during the exciting years when the United States was new. In the years after the American War of Independence, many people explored the wilderness west of the colonies, but no one made a longer or harder journey than these two young men from Virginia. They were the first to cross the thousands of miles of unknown land between the Mississippi River and the Pacific Ocean.

William Clark was the older of the two explorers. He was born in 1770. Many of the men in William's family were soldiers. One of his older brothers was George Rogers Clark, who was a hero of the American War of Independence. During that war, George Rogers Clark led the Americans in battles against the British and the Indians along the Ohio and Mississippi rivers, where the states of Ohio, Indiana, and Illinois are today. At that time, this was the far western frontier. After the war, William and the entire Clark family moved from Virginia to the valley of the Ohio River. The Clarks bought a farm in Kentucky when William was 14 years old.

William grew into a tall, strong, red-haired young man. He was at home in the woods, and he knew how to handle a boat on the river. This was an important skill on the frontier, where the rivers served as highways long before roads were

William Clark was born in Virginia in 1770. When Clark was a soldier at Fort Greenville, in Ohio, he became friends with Meriwether Lewis, who was also in the army there.

9

cut out of the thick forests. When William was about 21 years old, he joined the army. He fought the Indians in the Ohio and Indiana territories. At a post called Fort Greenville, in Ohio, he met a young soldier named Meriwether Lewis. The two men became good friends. When William Clark was 26 years old, he left the army and went to live at the family home in Louisville, Kentucky. But he had not seen the last of Meriwether Lewis.

Lewis was four years younger than Clark. He was born in 1774. His family's home was near Monticello, the home of Thomas Jefferson, the Virginia patriot who wrote the Declaration of Independence in 1776. Jefferson knew the young Meriwether and the whole Lewis family well. When Meriwether was five years old, his father died. His mother married again, and his new step-father moved the family to Georgia. Later, the stepfather died. Meriwether's mother moved back to Virginia with her children when Meriwether was 18.

Meriwether did not have much schooling, but he learned how to read and write. He read books on many subjects. He knew how to write letters and reports that were clear and lively. He also had an alert and intelligent mind. He loved to hike in the woods, and he was deeply curious about nature.

When he was 20 years old, Meriwether Lewis joined the army. He was sent to frontier forts along the Ohio River, where he met William Clark. He did well in the army and was made a captain. Perhaps Meriwether Lewis would have remained a frontier soldier for many years if his old neighbor Thomas Jefferson had not become president of the United States. But Jefferson had a grand plan for exploring the American West, and he chose Meriwether Lewis as his explorer.

Thomas Jefferson had been interested in the West for a long time. Even before he became president, he knew that the lands west of the Mississippi River would play a big part in the future of the United States. In the early years of the country, the Mississippi marked the edge of white settlement. Jefferson was curious to know what lay on the other side of it. A few traders and scouts

Meriwether Lewis was born in Virginia in 1774. After Thomas Jefferson became president, he asked Lewis to lead an expedition to explore the West.

had gone a little way into the wilderness and come back to tell of their adventures, but Jefferson wanted to send someone all the way across the country to the Pacific Ocean. No one had yet made such a journey.

In 1783, after the American War of Independence had ended, Jefferson asked George Rogers Clark, William Clark's older brother, to make the trip. At that time, the central region of North America was claimed by France. William's brother did not want to go into French lands. Later, Jefferson tried to help a French scientist who wanted to explore the wilderness, but that trip was never made. Then, in 1801, Jefferson became the third president of the United States.

One of the first things Jefferson did after becoming president was to make Meriwether Lewis his private secretary. Jefferson was still eager to learn about the wilderness beyond the frontier, and he wanted Lewis to lead an expedition of discovery. Around the same time, Jefferson read a book by a Scottish explorer named Alexander Mackenzie. This explorer had crossed Canada all the way to the Pacific Ocean. Mackenzie's book fired Jefferson's imagination. It made him see how vast and filled with wonders the wilderness was. It also made him want more than ever to send someone from the United States into the unknown American West.

Jefferson finally got his chance in 1803, the year he purchased the Louisiana Territory from France. The Louisiana Purchase was a treaty that gave the United States all the land between the Mississippi River and the Rocky Mountains. This meant that the territory that had once belonged to France was now part of the United States. Jefferson could then send an explorer out beyond the frontier, and the French would not stand in the way. The only things to fear were wild animals, hostile Indians, hunger, thirst, disease, and the other dangers of crossing thousands of miles of unexplored land.

Jefferson decided to send an expedition, or group of explorers, out west. He made Meriwether Lewis the captain of the expedition. He told Lewis to get men and supplies ready for the trip. Then he sent Lewis to Philadelphia, where some of the nation's most educated men lived. Lewis spent a month or so studying plants, animals, medicine, and astronomy with these learned men. He also bought supplies and had them shipped to Pittsburgh. He planned to take them from Pittsburgh down the Ohio River to the Mississippi River.

Before leaving for the frontier, Lewis told President Jefferson that he thought it would be a good idea if he shared the expedition with a second captain. Lewis wanted the other captain to be William Clark, his old friend from the army. Clark was a trained frontier soldier, and Lewis was sure he would be a good captain. So Lewis wrote to Clark, asking him to share the command. Clark accepted eagerly. President Jefferson also agreed, and Clark became the second captain of the expedition. The friendship between Lewis and Clark remained strong. They shared the command fairly, without quarrels or jealousy.

In 1803, Lewis was ready to set off for the

frontier. That June, Jefferson sent his final orders in a letter to Lewis. He told Lewis to keep careful records of everything the expedition saw and did. The explorers would be the first people to report on the huge new territory that had been added to the United States, and Jefferson wanted their report to be useful. He told them to study the plants, animals, minerals, rivers, mountains, and weather of the territory they crossed. He told them to take notes on the customs and languages of the Indian tribes they met. He told them also to make good maps so that other explorers and settlers could follow them.

Jefferson then told the explorers to search for a river route from the Mississippi River to the Pacific Ocean. Many people believed that a water passage from the Atlantic Ocean to the Pacific Ocean would be found through the continent of North America. This route already had a name, even though no one was sure whether it really existed. It was called the Northwest Passage. If a northwest passage did exist from the Mississippi to the Pacific, it would be a river highway that could open the West to settlers. It would also mean that American ships from New York and Boston could sail straight across the country to the Pacific Ocean. This would make it easier and cheaper for the United States to trade with China and other Asian countries. So Lewis and Clark were told to look for a northwest passage.

Meriwether Lewis left Washington in July 1803. He headed west to Pittsburgh. There he bought one boat and had another one built. Then he loaded the boats with his supplies and set off down the Ohio River. In October he arrived at the town of Clarksville, where William Clark was waiting to meet him. Lewis and Clark were reunited on the banks of the river. A few days later, the two captains set off down the Ohio toward the Mississippi River—and the mysteries that lie in wait beyond it.

The Corps of Discovery reached the frontier city of St. Louis in the fall of 1803. Lewis and Clark set up a camp nearby to enlist more men for the trip and to wait for winter to pass.

2
Getting
Started

Lewis and Clark made their way down the Ohio River as the year 1803 drew to a close. When they reached the place where the Ohio flows into the Mississippi River, they turned north and headed up the Mississippi. They went north as far as the frontier city of St. Louis. Just across the river from St. Louis, the Missouri River flows into the Mississippi from the western plains. Lewis and Clark planned to go up the Missouri as far as their boats would carry them. But it was now late fall. Before they could even start up the Missouri, they had to wait for winter to pass.

A little way outside St. Louis, Lewis and Clark built a fort for their winter headquarters. There they set about putting their expedition into shape. They called the expedition the Corps of Discovery. A few members of the Corps of Discovery had come from the East with Lewis. Clark had brought others from the woods of Kentucky and Ohio. But many members joined the Corps at St. Louis. Most of them were soldiers from nearby army posts. There were also some boatmen to help with the river journey. The captains hired some French Canadian traders and fur trappers who spoke the Indian languages. These men would be their guides and interpreters. The Corps of Discovery had one black member. He was named York, and he was Clark's slave. Altogether, Lewis and Clark had about 40 men under their command.

During the winter, Lewis spent a lot of time in St. Louis. He talked to fur traders and other people there, trying to learn all they knew about the Missouri River, the Indians, and the western lands. Clark took charge of training the men at the fort. He ordered them to get their boats, guns, and other gear ready for the next stage of the trip. Food was plentiful and the fort was comfortable enough, but by the time spring came, everyone was ready to begin their adventure.

On May 14, 1804, the Corps of Discovery started up the Missouri. People from St. Louis and the nearby farms came to stand on the banks of the river and to cheer on the brave travelers as they left.

In the first two weeks, the Corps passed some villages that had sprung up along the Missouri as Americans pushed farther into the frontier. The captains stopped at one of these settlements to buy extra supplies and to go to church. But before long they had passed the last little huddle of cabins. Ahead of them lay only the wilderness and the lonely river, their highway into Indian country.

Traveling the river was not easy. Because they were going upstream, they could not simply float along. Instead, the men had to row the boats or use poles to push against the river bottom. Sometimes they had to take ropes onto the banks and haul the boats up against the strong current. The river was tricky, too, filled with hidden dangers, such as fallen trees. And the sun grew hotter and more blistering every day as spring gave way to summer.

Still, the Corps of Discovery made progress up the Missouri. They were passing through fruitful country. Stands of cottonwood, linden, and walnut trees lined the riverbanks. The men who hunted game for the expedition's meals found plenty of deer and elk. But as Clark wrote in his journal, there were also plenty of troublesome ticks and mosquitoes.

By the end of August, the Corps had traveled up the river, past what are now the states of Missouri, Kansas, Nebraska, and Iowa. As they entered South Dakota, the men marveled at the strange new land that spread out around them. This was the High Plains country. Rugged cliffs and hills bordered the river. The cliffs were broken in places by steep, dry gullies. Beyond the cliffs, the plains stretched off to the hazy horizon. Now the explorers began to see the wildlife of the Far West. Herds of buffalo, numbering in the thousands, grazed in the distance. Hawks and eagles soared and wheeled high in the air. Pronghorn antelope bounded across the plains with astonishing speed. Closer at hand were the mounds and tunnels of prairie dogs, busy brown burrowers that Lewis called "barking squirrels." Lewis and Clark had truly entered a new world, and they found it wonderful.

They met Indians on their trip up the Missouri. President Jefferson had told Lewis to make friends with the Indians of the West, so Lewis had brought gifts of blankets, fishhooks, knives, mirrors, and silver medals for the Indians. But Lewis also had to tell the Indians that their land now belonged to the United States. Some of the Indians

*Lewis and Clark
often saw herds
of buffalo and
antelope grazing
on the plains or
drinking water in
the Missouri River.*

were interested in what the white men had to say. Many of them were friendly. They did not realize that thousands of white settlers and homesteaders would follow Lewis and Clark into the West, killing the buffalo and building farms on what the Indians considered to be *their* land. Some other Indian tribes were simply not interested in the Lewis and Clark expedition, and a few were unfriendly.

The worst moments came when Lewis and Clark visited the camp of a tribe called the Teton Sioux. These Indians lived near where the city of Pierre, South Dakota, stands today. They had

While making their way north and then west, the Corps beheld many kinds of wildlife they had never seen before. One delightful animal that was new to them was the prairie dog, or as Lewis called it, the "barking squirrel."

controlled trade among the Indian tribes along the Missouri River for a long time. They saw the white men as rivals and threatened to steal one of the expedition's boats. Lewis and Clark managed to avoid a fight. They even spent two evenings in the Indians' camp, but they did not feel that they had made friends with the Teton Sioux.

As they left the land of the Sioux, the captains hoped that things would be better farther up the river, where the Mandan and Hidatsa Indians lived. Lewis had learned from the fur traders that these tribes were friendly to whites. Because Lewis and Clark knew that they could not travel during the harsh months of winter, they wanted to spend the winter with the Mandan Indians. But it was already October. The leaves on the trees turned red and gold, and then they started to fall. The days grew shorter and colder. Traces of ice began to form on the edge of the river at night. Flocks of geese and ducks flew overhead, going south for the winter. The expedition could not keep on moving much longer.

A Hidatsa warrior clutches a bow and arrows. Lewis and Clark met the Hidatsas and their neighbors, the Mandan Indians, near present-day Bismarck, North Dakota.

CHAPTER

3

Winter with
the Indians

In the last days of October, the Corps of Discovery came upon the Mandan Indians and their neighbors, the Hidatsas. These 2 tribes lived in 5 villages along the Missouri River, about 50 miles north of where Bismarck, North Dakota, stands today. The Mandans and the Hidatsas knew about white people and their trade goods from meetings with French Canadian fur trappers and others who had ventured into their land. They were friendly to Lewis and Clark. The captains decided to spend the winter with these Indians.

The Corps built a fort near one of the Mandan villages.

Fort Mandan, as it was called, had high walls on the outside. On the inside were huts for the men and a shed to hold the supplies. The roof of the shed served as a watchtower, where a sentry stood guard. But the fort never came under attack. The winter passed peacefully. The Mandans and the Hidatsas were sociable, often visiting Fort Mandan. In turn, Lewis and Clark spent much time in the Indian villages. They tried to learn as much as they could about how the Indians lived, and they kept records of their discoveries in their journals.

Like most people of their time, Lewis and Clark took it for granted that the white man's way of life was better and more "civilized" than the Indian's way of life. So some of the captains' judgments about the Indians were prejudiced or overly harsh. (A prejudice is a judgment or opin-ion, usually unfriendly, that has been formed about something or someone before knowing the facts.) But many of the things they said about the Indians were fair-minded and true.

They found that the Mandans and the Hidatsas were farmers who grew corn, beans, and squash. Two or three times each year, the Indians, on horseback, hunted buffalo on the plains, pelting the shaggy beasts with arrows. Some men from the expedition went on one of the Mandan buffalo hunts, and they were filled with praise for the Indians' skilled horsemanship and marksmanship. The Indians lived in large, circular lodges with earthen walls. On cold nights they brought their dogs and horses into the lodges. They traveled the river in dugouts, which were boats hollowed out from large logs, and in smaller canoes. The captains planned to use some canoes in the spring when they started upriver again.

President Jefferson wanted Lewis and Clark to do more than study the Indians and report on their way of life. He also wanted them to explain to the tribes they met that the United States now held claim to their land under the

Louisiana Purchase. Jefferson hoped that the Lewis and Clark expedition would pave the way for good relations between the whites of the United States and the Indians of the Far West. He urged the captains to try to make peace between rival groups, such as the Mandans and the Sioux, so that the western plains would not be torn by tribal wars. And he hoped that Lewis and Clark could interest the Indians in trading with the Americans instead of the British, who now controlled Canada, or the Spanish, who controlled the American Southwest.

But Lewis and Clark found that the Mandans and the Hidatsas were not very interested in

The Mandans, who became friendly with the Corps, brought their dogs and horses inside their huts at night. Both the Mandans and the Hidatsas lived in round, earth-covered huts. Sometimes as many as 40 people lived in one hut.

politics. They were more interested in the day-to-day business of trade, and they were willing to deal with anyone who wanted to buy or sell. The Mandans and the Hidatsas were at the center of a huge Indian trade network. They traded with the western tribes for horses, furs, and skins. Then they traded these items with the eastern tribes for guns and goods that the Indians of the East got from the whites.

The Hidatsas were more warlike than were the Mandans. Hidatsa warriors sometimes went as far west as the Rocky Mountains to raid other tribes. This made them a good source of information about the routes that led west, where Lewis and Clark wanted to go. During their time at Fort Mandan, Lewis and Clark asked the Indians many questions about the western routes and tribes. They wanted to know as much as they could about the upper Missouri River and the Rocky Mountains. The captains used what they learned from the Indians to plan the next stage of the trip. Lewis and Clark also added new members to the Corps of Discovery at Fort Mandan.

They hired several French traders who had come down into Indian country from Canada. These men knew the Indian languages and would be useful as interpreters. One of the French Canadians was named Toussaint Charbonneau. He had an Indian wife named Sacagawea. She was a member of the Shoshone tribe that lived in the Rocky Mountains, but she had been kidnapped by the Hidatsas a few years earlier. Lewis and Clark agreed that Sacagawea could join the expedition. They wanted her to be their interpreter when they met the Shoshones. During the winter, Sacagawea bore a son to Charbonneau. Jean Baptiste, as the baby was named, became the youngest member of the Corps of Discovery. His mother carried him on her back while they traveled.

The Lewis and Clark expedition spent five months at Fort Mandan. Although winter on the northern plains was often bitterly cold, with temperatures as low as 40 degrees below zero, the men were in good spirits. They celebrated Christmas and New Year's Day with music and dancing. And they ate well. Hunters went out often to keep

Indians gather on a bluff of the Rocky Mountains. In July 1805, Lewis and Clark reached the foothills of the towering Rockies.

the Corps supplied with fresh meat. In a single day, the Corps could eat an entire buffalo or four deer. The men also traded axes and other metal objects for vegetables from the Indians' winter stores. The whites and the Indians visited each other's camps almost every day. York, Clark's slave, was a welcome visitor in the Indian villages. The Indians were amazed by him because they had never seen a black person. One Hidatsa chief rubbed York's skin with a wet finger, trying to remove what he thought was black paint.

As spring drew on, the ice that had choked the river all winter began to melt. By April the river was flowing freely once again. The nights were still cold, but the weather no longer kept the men caged inside the fort. It was time for the expedition to move on.

Before they left Fort Mandan, the captains sent a dozen or so men back down the Missouri River to St. Louis with messages for President Jefferson. This return party took the largest and heaviest boat. The captains knew that such a boat would be of little use farther upstream, where the river would become narrower and rougher.

The return party carried the journals and notebooks of the two captains, with all the information they had gathered up to that point. These journals were to be sent to the president in Washington. Lewis and Clark also sent samples of new plants they had discovered on the plains, the skins of several animals, and a live prairie dog. Clark had drawn a very thorough map of the territory that the expedition had covered, and this was sent back to Jefferson, too. Finally, the return party carried letters to family and friends from the men of the Corps.

On April 7, 1805, Lewis and Clark said good-bye to the members of the return party and to the Indians who had been their neighbors all winter. With a total of 33 people, including the captains, York, Sacagawea, and Jean Baptiste, the Corps of Discovery set out north and then west, up the Missouri River into a region where no whites had gone before.

The expedition traveled in two dugouts and six small canoes. Lewis and Clark hoped to find a way through the Rocky Mountains, reach the edge of the Pacific, and then make their way back through the mountains and down the river to Fort Mandan—all before winter set in again in six months or so. They did not know how many obstacles they would meet, but they knew that they had to get out of the mountains before the snow fell. To be trapped in the mountains in winter would mean certain death.

Some travelers in the West consult their Indian guide.
Lewis and Clark depended a lot on the information
that the Indians gave them about the countryside
around them.

4

Crossing
the Rockies

After leaving the Mandan and Hidatsa country,
the Lewis and Clark expedition followed the Missouri River north and then west. They were passing through what is now the state of North
Dakota. Then, at the point where the Yellowstone
River flows into the Missouri River, the expedition crossed into present-day Montana. The captains were still following the Missouri. Soon they
entered a dry, rugged region now called the Bad-
lands, not far from the Canadian border.

During their crossing of the Rockies, Lewis and Clark reported seeing fierce grizzly bears like the ones pictured here.

Every day there were strange and exciting new sights. At one place where the river ran between sheer cliffs of black and white stone, Lewis wrote that the cliffs looked like rows of giant buildings standing in the middle of the wilderness. Both captains described plants and birds unlike any they had seen before. They also reported seeing new animals. Bighorn sheep and Rocky Mountain sheep scrambled up the stony bluffs and leapt from crag to crag on the cliffs above

the river. Lewis and Clark were the first white people to see these sheep. They marveled at their gracefulness. But the animal that interested them most was the grizzly bear.

The captains had heard stories about the huge, fierce grizzlies from the Indians. Lewis said in his journal that when the Indians went out to hunt for grizzly bears, they prepared just as if they were going to war with an enemy tribe. At first Lewis did not believe that the bears could be as fearsome as the Indians said. But some terrifying encounters with bears changed his mind. One bear swam halfway across the river after the men—even though it had been shot 10 times. Another wounded bear chased one of the soldiers for more than half a mile. Lewis then admitted that he would rather fight two Indians than one grizzly bear. But one day when he was out hunting alone, a grizzly came after him. Lewis tried to shoot, only to find that he had forgotten to load his rifle. He ran back to the river with the bear at his heels. Plunging into the water, Lewis made ready to defend himself with a spear. He probably could not have stopped the grizzly with only a spear, but he was lucky that day. The bear lost interest. It turned and tromped away.

The Corps found signs of Indians along the way. Once Lewis and Clark saw a big pile of buffalo carcasses at the base of a steep cliff. They knew that the Indians who lived nearby had driven the buffalo over the cliff to kill them. But although they saw many large, well-fed wolves prowling among the carcasses, they did not see the Indians.

As the days passed, travel became more difficult. The river grew shallower and swifter, and there were rapids. The weather was also unpredictable. At first the expedition was lashed by the snow squalls of spring. Then thunderstorms brought cold rain and large hailstones that were sharp enough to draw blood. High winds blew stinging sand at the travelers. Once a sudden gust of wind turned one of the dugouts on its side. Both captains were ashore at the time. Charbonneau was in the dugout, but he was too frightened to do anything to help save it. Luckily, another boatman was able to get the dugout to the riverbank before it sank. But the heroine of the day was Sacagawea, who had been riding in the dugout when it almost overturned. She calmly held on to little Jean Baptiste with one hand, and with the other hand she scooped up many of the items that had fallen from the dugout into the river. Lewis wrote in his journal that he was grateful to her, because the loss of any of the expedition's tools or supplies could have been a tragedy.

In June the expedition arrived at a series of waterfalls where Great Falls, Montana, stands today. The travelers had to carry their supplies and boats by land for 18 miles around these falls. Carrying boats and goods around an obstacle in a river is called portaging, and it can be very hard work. It took the Corps of Discovery a month of backbreaking labor to build wagons, clear tracks, and haul their heavy loads around the falls. Lewis knew that they would not be able to reach the Pacific Ocean and come back again before winter. Now he just hoped that they could make it through the Rockies and to the other side before winter.

In July the Corps of Discovery entered the foothills of the mountains. This was land that Sacagawea recognized. It was the homeland of her people, the Shoshones. One night they camped on the very spot from which she had been kidnapped years before. But they did not meet any

Indians. So they went on, following smaller and smaller streams and then working their way higher into the mountains on foot. Finally, in August, Lewis and a group of the men met a group of Shoshones. It turned out that the Shoshone chief, Cameahwait, was Sacagawea's brother. Because of this kinship, the Shoshones treated the travelers from the East as friends. The Indians sold the captains some horses. They also told Lewis and Clark about the trails and passes through the mountains. When the expedition moved on, it was led by a Shoshone guide. The explorers called him Old Toby.

Lewis and Clark now faced the hardest part of their journey: crossing the Continental, or Great, Divide. The Continental Divide is the highest point on the continent. In North America this point is in the Rocky Mountains. The Rocky Mountains are not a single mountain range. They are a collection of many ranges that form a mighty chain of mountains, dividing North America into two parts. Lewis and Clark had to cross a section

The salmonberry, a red-flowered raspberry, was discovered by Lewis. Every day, Lewis and Clark wrote about their findings and made detailed drawings of the plants, trees, and birds they saw.

Tab. 16. p.

Rubus spectabilis.

of the Rockies called the Bitterroot Range, along the border between what are now the states of Montana and Idaho.

For most of September, the Corps of Discovery labored up and down narrow, winding trails in the Bitterroots. They crossed the Continental Divide at a place called the Lolo Pass. At last they began to climb down from the mountains on a trail that the Indians called the Lolo Trail. But climbing down was even more difficult and dangerous than climbing up had been. Snow was falling in the high country, and the trail was treacherous. Some of the packhorses slipped and fell to their death, carrying supplies with them.

Yet Lewis and Clark still obeyed Jefferson's orders. Each day they took notes on the plants, trees, and birds they saw in the mountains. But they also wrote in their journals that everyone was wet, cold, and hungry. Game was scarce. Soon the travelers had to kill and eat as many of their horses as they could spare. By the time they were almost out of the mountains, they were in desperate trouble.

When Lewis and Clark saw Mount Hood, the highest peak in Oregon, they knew they were coming to a region that had earlier been visited by British and American sailors.

CHAPTER

5
The Pacific Ocean

When the Corps had nearly run out of food, Clark went ahead with a few men to scout for Indians who might be able to help. On a plain west of the mountains they found a camp of the Nez Percé Indians. The Nez Percés lived on fish, mainly salmon, and on the roots of a plant called camas. (One member of the expedition wrote in his diary that the camas roots reminded him of pumpkins.) They shared these supplies with the whites. With the help of the Nez Percés, the entire expedition was soon out of the mountains and comfortably fed.

Lewis and Clark met with the Nez Percé chief near where the city of Orofino, Idaho, is now located. The captains asked how they could reach the Columbia River. This mighty river flows down from Canada through the state of Washington into the Pacific Ocean. Sea captains from Spain, Britain, and the United States had explored the mouth of the river from the ocean. European and American ships had come there to trade with the local Indians for the furs of seals and sea otters. Some of these sea captains had made maps of the Pacific coast, and Clark had brought these maps with him. He and Lewis knew that if they could reach the Columbia, the river would carry them to the coast.

From the Indians they learned that a nearby river, which the captains called the Clearwater, would take them to the Snake River. The Snake River, in turn, would take them to the Columbia. So now, after crossing the mountains on foot, the Corps of Discovery returned to the water for the final stage of its outward journey.

The men felled trees and made five dugouts. They left their horses with the Nez Percés, to be picked up again on their return journey. Then, on October 7, the expedition set out for the Pacific. Before, when they traveled up the Missouri, they had been going against the current. Now they were going in the same direction as the river, and progress was swift. They had to portage around some rapids, and they sometimes stopped to trade for food with the local Indians, but they reached the Columbia River in little more than a week.

The passage down the Columbia was rougher than the captains had thought it would be. They ran into a 55-mile-long stretch of waterfalls and churning rapids. They tried to portage, but the river ran between high, steep canyon walls, and there was nowhere to walk. So the travelers had to stay in their wildly whirling boats and ride out the rapids. The local Indians looked on in amazement, but all the explorers made it safely through the swirling water.

After the rapids, the river grew broader and quieter. The dry, barren lands on both sides of the river gave way to lush green forests. Before long, Lewis and Clark saw some high, snow-capped mountains in the distance. They believed that these were the peaks that had been spotted from the sea by earlier explorers of the coast. Next the captains saw that some of the Indians were wearing bits of factory-made clothing that must have come from trade with British or American ships. Then they even heard some Indians cursing in English. All of these signs told the captains that they were getting close to their goal at last.

On November 7, 1805, the travelers reached the long, broad estuary, or mouth, of the Columbia River. Still in their boats, they made their way along the north side of this wide stretch of water. Then, on November 15, the Lewis and Clark expedition arrived at the shore of the Pacific Ocean. The men felt triumphant. They had survived the first continental crossing. Many of them proudly carved their name in the bark of trees.

They were eager to return to St. Louis and tell the world of their success, but first they had to wait out the winter.

The captains asked their followers where they thought the winter camp should be built. Everyone in the expedition, including York and Sacagawea, had a vote. The site that was chosen was on the south bank of the Columbia River, near where the city of Astoria, Oregon, is today. A wooden fort was built in the shape of a square, with seven rooms on the inside. The captains shared one room. Charbonneau, Sacagawea, and their son had a room. The rest of the men shared the other five rooms. The fort was named Fort Clatsop, after the Indian tribe that lived on the south side of the river. A tribe called the Chinooks lived on the north side.

The Pacific coast was not as cold as the country around Fort Mandan had been. But the winter weather was dreary and damp. Almost every day brought rain and fog. Here game was not as abundant as on the central plains, and the hunters sometimes had a hard time keeping the cooks supplied with elk, deer, and game birds. When meat was scarce, the travelers ate what the Indians ate: roots and herbs, dried fish, and dog meat.

By this time the expedition had been away from St. Louis for almost two years. The journals show that some members of the Corps thought often about the delicious meals they planned to eat as soon as they returned home. On New Year's Day, January 1, 1806, Lewis wrote about how much he was looking forward to eating "civilized" food once again.

Lewis and Clark did not admire the Chinook and Clatsop Indians. The people of these tribes were used to trading with the ships that called from time to time for furs, so they drove a hard bargain when they sold food to the white men. The Indians also stole some items from the whites, causing Lewis and Clark to complain that the coast Indians were untrustworthy. All in all, the captains felt that the Chinooks and the Clat-

A Chinook mother holds her baby in a special wooden
cradle that is designed to flatten its forehead. Some
Indian tribes in the Northwest believed that a long
forehead was a sign of importance.

sops compared poorly to the noble and generous Mandans, Hidatsas, Shoshones, and Nez Percés. Lewis and Clark discouraged the men from having any dealings with the Chinooks and the Clatsops, and no Indian was allowed in the fort after sundown. Fort Clatsop was quite different from Fort Mandan, where Indians had visited on most evenings.

Much work was done during the winter. The men of the Corps had to clean and repair their equipment for the homeward journey. They also had to make clothing out of elk skin. Footwear was especially important, because the rocky paths through the mountains could wear out a pair of leather shoes in a few days. By the end of the winter, the men had made 338 pairs of moccasins for the trip home.

Another task that kept the Corps busy was salt making. They needed salt to make their boring diet taste better and also to keep their meat from spoiling. The best way to get salt was to boil seawater. After the water boiled away, salt remained. So a salt camp was set up on the coast about 15 miles southwest of the fort. Teams of three or four men at a time took turns on duty there. In January, Clark led a group of 13 men, together with Sacagawea and Jean Baptiste, to the coast near the salt camp to see the huge carcass of a whale that had become stranded on the beach. The Indians were butchering the whale, and they sold some whale meat and whale oil to Clark.

Lewis and Clark spent the winter updating their notes. Lewis wrote long, detailed descriptions of the plants, animals, and Indians he had seen on his way from the Rocky Mountains to the sea. Clark copied all of Lewis's notes into his own journal. That way, if something happened to one set of notes, the information would still have a chance of reaching President Jefferson. But Clark's main job was mapmaking. He drew a number of good maps showing the route west from Fort Mandan to the Pacific. The captains hoped to send their journals and maps back to the eastern United States on an American ship. But no ships called at the mouth of the Columbia River during the winter of 1805–6.

By March, everyone tired of Fort Clatsop. The captains were as eager as anyone to start for

Lewis drew this picture of a coho, or silver salmon, in his journal on March 16, 1806. Clark copied all of Lewis's entries in his own diary in order to give the Corps' discoveries a good chance of making their way back to the president.

home. After all, their job was only half-done. They had crossed the continent, but they still had to get word of their discoveries back to Jefferson and the people of the United States.

Before Lewis and Clark could leave the coast, they had to solve a problem about the boats. Only three of the expedition's five dugouts were in good condition. Two more boats were needed for the journey upriver. The Clatsops had boats to sell, but their price was high. One Indian traded a boat for Lewis's fancy uniform jacket. Then, in their hurry to depart, the captains told one of their men to steal an Indian boat. Although the order to steal went against army rules, the captains felt that the boat was equal payment for the six elk the Clatsops had previously stolen from the Corps' hunters. The boat was taken, and the expedition left Fort Clatsop on March 23, 1806. On the day they departed, Clark wrote in his journal that they had lived as well at Fort Clatsop "as we had any right to expect."

The Corps obtained two elaborately carved Indian canoes, like the ones shown here, for their journey back home.

CHAPTER

6

The Long
Road Home

For the first part of the homebound trip, the expedition went back up the Columbia River. The explorers had covered this territory before but still made some new discoveries along the way. Clark spent two days scouting along the Willamette River, which flows into the Columbia near present-day Portland, Oregon. He and Lewis were impressed by the fertile Willamette Valley. Lewis later reported that it was the best place for settlers on the west side of the Rocky Mountains. Because of this good report, many settlers from the East came to the Willamette Valley in the 1840s. Today it is still the most settled part of Oregon.

The Corps went on up the river, wearily portaging around falls and rapids. The men had to buy food from the river Indians, and they grew tired of bargaining. Once there was a serious quarrel when some Indians stole a few items from the expedition. Clark warned the Indians that he could kill them and burn their villages if they made him angry. The stolen goods were returned.

Instead of taking their canoes all the way to the mountains, the explorers traded the canoes for horses and followed the course of the Columbia River on land. At the end of April they met a friendly group of Walula Indians, who held a large feast for the visitors. After the feast, the whites and the Indians danced together all night to the sound of Indian drums.

The Walulas told Lewis of a short land route to the Nez Percé region. So instead of following the course of the Snake River, as they had done on the outward trip, the Corps of Discovery took the Indian route from the Columbia. It led to a Nez Percé camp near the Clearwater River.

By now it was the middle of May. The valleys were warm, but the captains were disappointed to learn from the Indians that snow still blanketed the high passes. The Indians warned them that it was much too soon to try to cross the Bitterroot Range.

The expedition spent more than a month camped with the Nez Percés, waiting for the trail through the mountains to be clear of snow. During that time the captains studied the local geography and plant life. They also wrote many pages of notes about the Nez Percés, whom they admired.

At last, in late June, the Corps set out into the mountains with three Nez Percé guides. This time they crossed the pass easily in only six days— a great improvement over the dangerous descent of the year before.

When they reached a campsite in the mountains near the present-day city of Missoula, Montana, the captains split the expedition in two. This was something they had planned during the winter. They wanted to explore more of what is now Montana on their way home. They were especially eager to explore some of the tributaries, or smaller rivers, that flowed into the Missouri. The Louisiana Purchase had given the United States all the land around every river that flowed into the Mississippi River. Because the Missouri poured into the Mississippi, all of the rivers and streams that gushed into the Missouri on its way to the Mississippi were now part of the United States. Lewis and Clark wanted to explore some of these tributaries to see how far America's claim spread.

Lewis's group planned to stay close to the Missouri River. This would be almost the same route that the expedition had taken earlier on its westward trip. But along the way, Lewis would explore some of the rivers that flowed into the Missouri from the north. Clark's group planned to follow a more southerly route through Montana. Clark would head south through the fringes of the mountains until he found the Yellowstone

River, which was also a tributary of the Missouri. Then he would follow the Yellowstone east to where it meets the Missouri. There his group and Lewis's group would be reunited.

The two captains parted on July 3. Lewis's journey proved to be the more adventurous trip. When he took two men for a scouting trek up a river he named the Marias, he ran into a group of Blackfoot Indians, a rather fierce, warlike tribe. They were the enemies of the Shoshones and the Nez Percés, and the explorers had been very glad not to meet any of them on the way west. Lewis's encounter with them turned violent when the Indians tried to steal the explorers' rifles and horses. One Indian was stabbed to death in a fight over the rifles, and Lewis shot and killed another who was trying to snatch the horses. The dying Indian fired a last shot at Lewis and just missed the captain's head. After this struggle, Lewis and the other two men rode as fast as they could back to the Missouri, hoping that they would not be attacked by another band of angry Blackfoot Indians on the way. Lewis reached the river safely and took his whole group downstream in canoes.

Meanwhile, Clark and his team were making their way along a confusing maze of Indian trails that twisted through the mountains and valleys of southwestern Montana. Sacagawea was a good guide for this part of the trip. Clark let her pick the trails to follow, and he wrote in his journal that she had been a great help. The explorers reached the Yellowstone River on July 15. They

built canoes from cottonwood trees and then launched themselves on the river.

Clark's river journey was fairly uneventful. The captain kept careful notes and measurements of the river's course so that he could draw a good map of it. The men went hunting at every stop. Now that they were in the High Plains again, they could once more hunt for buffalo, and they rejoiced in the taste of buffalo stews and steaks. They saw herds that were miles long—thousands

A group of Indians camp near the Rockies. Lewis and Clark greatly admired the Nez Percés and studied their way of life closely.

upon thousands of animals, stirring up vast clouds of dust. There were so many buffalo on the plains that Clark was afraid the men would be trampled. And at night the explorers were kept awake by the snorts and grunts of the buffalo.

Clark's team was the first to reach the place where the Yellowstone meets the Missouri. Clark left a note there for Lewis and then went a short distance down the Missouri. Lewis arrived at the mouth of the Yellowstone four days later, on August 7, and found the note. His team caught up with Clark's team on August 12.

Two days later, the explorers arrived at the villages of the Mandan and Hidatsa Indians, where they had spent the winter of 1804–5. They held council meetings with the chiefs. But by now everyone wanted to finish the last leg of the trip home, so the Corps of Discovery again set sail down the Missouri on August 17. When the Corps sailed, Charbonneau, Sacagawea, and Jean Baptiste stayed behind in their Indian home. One of the soldiers also stayed behind. His name was

John Colter. The expedition had met some fur trappers entering the Mandan country, and the trappers wanted Colter to go back up the river with them as their guide. The captains gave Colter permission to leave the expedition. Colter went on to become the first of a hardy breed of western guides and trappers who were called mountain men. Like Lewis and Clark before them, the mountain men explored the West and helped open it up to settlers.

In the last stages of their journey on the Missouri, Lewis and Clark met some traders who were headed up the river. They learned from these men that most people in the United States had long ago given the explorers up for lost. After all, they had been gone for two and a half years. But Clark was happy to hear that President Jefferson had not given up hope. He still believed that the captains might return.

The Lewis and Clark expedition arrived in St. Louis on September 23, 1806. Bells rang and people fired their guns into the air with joy. The

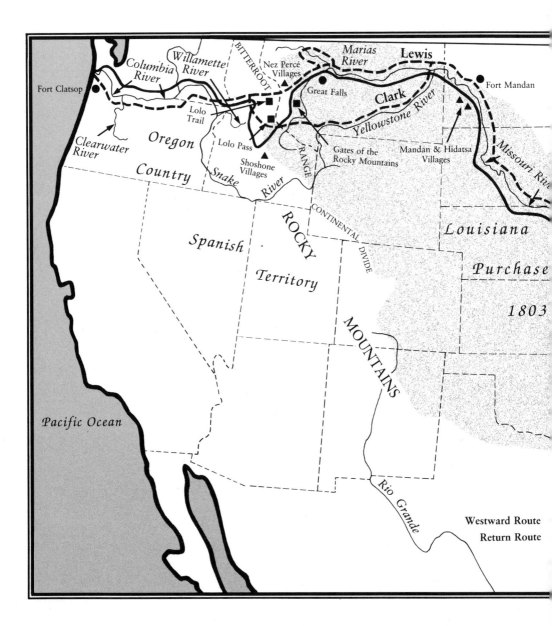

Fort Clatsop

Columbia
River

Willamette
River

BITTERROOT

Nez Percé
Villages

Marias
River

Lewis

Fort Mandan

Clearwater
River

Oregon

Lolo
Trail

Great Falls

Clark

Yellowstone River

Country

Lolo Pass

Shoshone
Villages

Gates of the
Rocky Mountains

Mandan & Hidatsa
Villages

Missouri River

Snake

River

RANGE

Louisiana

CONTINENTAL

ROCKY

Spanish

DIVIDE

Purchase

Territory

1803

MOUNTAINS

Pacific Ocean

Rio Grande

Westward Route

Return Route

LEWIS and CLARK'S ROUTE

This map shows the routes taken by Lewis and Clark on their way to the Pacific Ocean and back. The entire journey lasted 28 months and covered more than 8,000 miles.

same townspeople who had rooted for the explorers in 1804 now lined the riverbanks to cheer them into town. The first thing Lewis did when they reached St. Louis was to write a letter to President Jefferson. He told the president that the expedition had succeeded in its mission: Lewis and Clark had crossed the American continent.

Lewis and Clark's Corps of Discovery was not only the first expedition to cross the American West, but it was also one of the most successful exploring missions of all time. In almost two and a half years, the expedition covered about 8,000 miles, most of it unknown territory. Only one man was lost—a soldier who had died of appendicitis. The expedition did not find the Northwest Passage, because there is no such water route. But the Corps of Discovery did bring back hundreds of pages of useful information about the West and detailed maps that helped later travelers and settlers find their way. All of this information was welcome to the people of the United States, who were very curious about their new western territories. When a book about the trip based on the captains' journals was published in 1814, it became a best-seller.

The two heroes of the expedition had very different fates. In 1806, Meriwether Lewis was appointed governor of the Louisiana Territory by President Jefferson. Three years later, Lewis died in Tennessee from a gunshot wound he mysteriously received while on his way to Washington. But William Clark lived in St. Louis for many years. In 1813, he became the governor of the Missouri Territory that he had explored. Later, he was the U.S. government's superintendent of Indian affairs. Clark named his oldest son Meriwether Lewis Clark in honor of his friend. He also kept a promise to Sacagawea and made sure that her son, Jean Baptiste, got a good education.

William Clark died in St. Louis in 1838. But he and Meriwether Lewis, two Virginians who crossed a continent for their president, live on in history as heroic explorers, outstanding scientists, and great leaders.

Chronology

1770	William Clark is born in Virginia.
1774	Meriwether Lewis is born in Virginia.
1792–93	Scottish explorer Alexander Mackenzie crosses North America from east to west in what is now Canada.
1790s	Lewis and Clark serve together in the army at frontier forts along the Ohio River.
1801	Thomas Jefferson becomes president; Jefferson makes Lewis his private secretary.
1802	Jefferson reads Alexander Mackenzie's account of his journey.

1803	Jefferson purchases the Louisiana Territory from France, and the United States gains the territory between the Mississippi River and the Rocky Mountains; Lewis and Clark are made captains of an expedition to cross the American West.
1804	Lewis and Clark set out from a camp near St. Louis on May 14 with about 40 men; the expedition spends the winter of 1804–5 with the Mandan Indians in North Dakota.
1805	The expedition enters the Rocky Mountains in July and comes out on the western side in September; Lewis and Clark reach the Pacific Ocean coast in Oregon on November 15; the expedition spends the winter of 1805–6 in a camp in Oregon.
1806	The expedition sets out for home in March; the explorers and their men reach St. Louis on September 23.
1809	Lewis dies in Tennessee.
1814	A book about the expedition based on the captains' journals is published.
1838	Clark dies in St. Louis.

Glossary

astronomy   the study of space and the stars; in Lewis and Clark's time, people used the positions of the stars to establish directions and to determine their own locations

continent   a large land mass; Earth has seven continents: North America, South America, Europe, Asia, Africa, Australia, and Antarctica

Continental Divide   the highest point on the continent; in North America, the Continental Divide, also called the Great Divide, is situated in the Rocky Mountains and divides all of the rivers so that water on one side of the Divide flows east, toward the Atlantic Ocean, and water on the other side flows west, toward the Pacific Ocean

corps   a group of people working together for a special purpose

estuary   the bay or inlet that is formed where a river flows into the sea

expedition   a journey or trip with a goal, usually to explore new places; the word *expedition* can also be used for the group of people who are making the journey

interpreter a person who speaks two or more languages; with the help of an interpreter, two people who do not speak each other's language can communicate: The interpreter listens to what each one says and then tells it to the other person in that person's language

journal a diary or notebook

Northwest Passage an imaginary water route between the Atlantic and Pacific oceans that many explorers looked for along the northern coast of North America but could not find because it does not exist

portage a place where a river is blocked by rapids, waterfalls, or some other barrier; people who are traveling by boat cannot get through and must use a *portage*, or passage on land around the barrier; *portaging* means carrying goods, and sometimes even canoes or boats, around the barriers in a river or a stream

territory a stretch of land; a territory might be a certain place, as in "the territory claimed by the United States," or it might just mean a large area, as in "the unknown territory in the West"

tributary a river that feeds, or flows into, a larger river; for example, the Missouri River is a tributary of the Mississippi River, and the Yellowstone River is a tributary of the Missouri River

Index

Rebecca Stefoff is a Philadelphia-based writer and editor. She holds a Ph.D. in English from the University of Pennsylvania, where she taught for three years. Ms. Stefoff is the author of more than 30 biographies and nonfiction books for young people and has served as the editorial director of the Chelsea House series LET'S DISCOVER CANADA.

Picture Credits